Euphonic Melodies

Caressing you soul

Esha Mahajan

TITLE- Euphonic Melodies

Author: Esha Mahajan

First Published by Hatchegg Publication2022
ISBN: 978-93-90446-72-8
Price: Rs. 299/-
Hatchegg Publication
{Imprint: Manda Publishers}
info.hatcheggpublication@gmail.com
www.hatcheggpublication.com
+91 8766355652
Cover Design:
Aryan
Image source: shutterstock.com {licensed image}

Distributed by:
Amazon, Flipkart, Hatchegg Publication

Printing by:
Thomson Press

About the Book

“Euphonic Melodies, caressing your soul” is a book which has the poems which will be feast to your soul and heart. It is imbibed with positive thoughts and will surely bring a positive change in your life.

It will bring a smile on your face as it will appeal to your different moods. It’s a collection of love poems, which will caress your heart and will take you to the romantic world, optimistic poems, will kindle the spirit of hopefulness in your life, nature related poems, will make you a nature lover, spiritual poems, will take you to the pilgrimage, passionate poems will make you follow your passion, soulful poems, will take you to the voyage with your soul, humanity related poems will make you think about your role as a human being, and there are many more.

In this book you will get a chance to meet a budding poet, my son, Reyansh Mahajan of 9years. His poems are based on his experiences and will take you to the dreamland where you will surely enjoy the adventurous rides and will recall your childhood pranks. You will really enjoy his poems and will love his rhymes.

In brief this book will take you to the journey with your own self and will surely make you think positively about this world and about yourself.

So read the poems of this book with your heart and soul, As it will help you to achieve life's actual goal.

Esha Mahajan is a teacher by profession but poet by heart. She is Masters in English and Masters in Education. She is married to Arun Mahajan, a businessman and is blessed with a son Reyansh Mahajan. She belongs to a small city Pathankot of Punjab. Reading and writing poems has always been an indispensable part of her life since her school days. She is a wonderful writer, an eloquent orator and a quick learner. She always tries to learn from each and everything and person around her. She is very optimistic and love to live the life to its fullest. Being sensitive and emotional by nature, she could actually empathise with other's conditions and could feel their pain. She is a good observer of people's behaviour which is visible in her writings. She believes in actual happiness which one can get by helping others. She believes in Karma Chakra which means "Whatever we give to the people of God, it will come back to us with interest"

Soulful poems

Positive thoughts

Thoughts we create in our mind,
Creates a world for us of that kind.

Positive thoughts build a divine halo around us,
Which strengthens our heart and soul to live in this cosmos.

Its magnetic effect attracts everything good towards it,
And repels whatever is harrowing, even a little bit.

It brings a natural glow on our face,
As it empowers us with God's divine grace.

It helps us to see good among all,
Which saves us from all sort of brawls.

It helps us to focus on our work,
As it keeps our mind and heart free of profane dust.

It makes us sympathetic and compassionate,
And enables us to perceive the emotions of all the animates.

It free our mind and heart from all sort of burden,
And enables us to show our new improved version.

It prepares us to face life's hurdles,
And protects us from pernicious infernal,

It brings happiness in our life,
As it enables us to discern God's guidelines.

It enables us to bring the shower of
exhilaration in his people's heart,

And helps them to understand that it's never
too late to restart.

It helps us to kindle the spirit of hope and love
in this world,
Which has now become the place of tyrant
and absurd.

Let's try to create the positive world for us,
Where we and our descendants will live
without any fuss.

Self-respect

Self-respect is respecting the soul within us,
Which guides us to keep ourselves away from the disgust.

Self-respect is the revering the ideals of our parents,
Who renounce their desires to make our life fluorescent.

Self-respect is celebrating the beautiful life without any fear,
And exploring it's hidden truth as a pioneer.

It takes years to make an ideal identity,
So it should not be put on stake for an enmity and an amenity.

Respect other's ideals and individuality,
And don't do anything which will harm their personality.

No one can bear the pain, if his soul is hurt,
As it's like the magma of emotions has burst.

It's the law of nature, whatever we give, the same we get,

So spread the flowers of love and end all the hatred.

Self-love

Self-love is loving the most beautiful creation of the creator,
Whom we usually see in the glass reflector.

The value of that creation is mostly ignored by us,
As we think in any situation, they can easily adjust.

We never give importance to his likes and dislikes,
As we always think of giving others splendid delights.

We mostly ignore his feelings and passions,
As we are always busy in responding to other's actions.

We never think of fulfilling his dreams,
As we are preoccupied in making others gleam.

We never think of his satisfaction,
But he spends his resources in making other's mansion.

We never do anything to bring happiness in his life,
But he is always there to end other's strifes.

We never think of exploring his creativity,
As he is always busy in upgrading other's productivity.

We never think of his health,
But he's always there in empowering other's strength.

Let's accept our love for this beautiful creator,
let's do something for our own leisure.

let's embellish ourselves with positive thoughts,
Which will bring an aura on our face, of divine gloss.

Let's accept the value of our feelings and passions,

Which will help us in fulfilling our ambitions.

Let's break the rigid rules and fly in the fresh air,
So that our wings could tear through the despair.

Let's live for ourselves at least once,
So that we could listen to our own heart's impulse.

let's learn

Let's learn how to live a life,
Not from others but from our own positive vibes,

Every creature teaches us something,
How to crawl and how to use our magical wings,

Every person we met, leaves his impact,
And it's up to us how do we react.

Even the mountains, rivers and forests,
Teaches us the lesson of helping God's creators,

Every positive thought we create,
Can bring in our life a huge change.

It will create an ambrosial aura around us,
Which will save us from the hideous disgust.

Nothing in this world teaches us hatred,
It's the creation of man's own filthy mind, which is no more sacred.

God created this earth for His beautiful creation,
But we are destroying it in our own frustration.

Let's merge our positive energy with the cosmic one,
So that we could again create a blissful world for everyone.

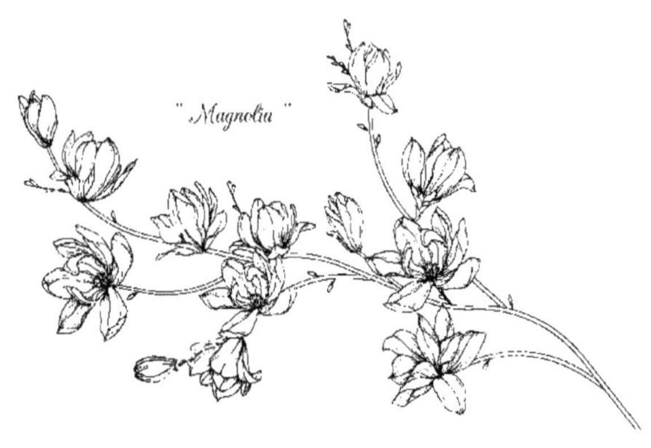

Inner strength

God has empowered us with seraphic powers,
Of overcoming all the hurdles to reach the success tower,
But being engrossed in our mundane regime,
We have forgotten the potential of His divine gleam.

No one can disturb the inner peace of humans,
As he is blessed with the ability to create illusions,
Using which he can make an armour for him,
And can save himself from all sort of profane grim.

No one can give us happiness,
As it's our own strength which keep us away from scrappiness,

We feel it when we, are able to connect with our creator,
As only then, we can fight with ominous demons like a crusader.

No one can hurt us,
Except our own absurd fuss,
It's the unfulfillment of our expectations,
Which is the main reason of our depressing relations.

No one can make us furious,
Without the permission of our mind, imperious,
No one is strong enough to intrude in our personal space,
Till the time we allow him to make us deface.

So, let's go on a divine voyage with our heavenly soul,
It will enable us to know our divine goal,
Will help us to fathom its eternal depth,
So that we can actually know our inner strength.

Knowledge

Knowledge is what, that differs us from animals,
It makes us magnanimous and radical,
It has the power to change the world,
And can save it's animaties from the dreadful scourge.

It has no beginning and no ending,
The more we learn, the more we start comprehending,
It has mystical powers of hiding our flaws,
And helps us to get from everyone, a round of applause.

It makes us distinct from the common crowd,
As it makes our thoughts, intense and profound,
Using which, we can dive into our own soul,
And can find out the precious and pearled goals.

It enables us to fulfill our dreams,
Though for that, we have to follow a tough regime,
It gives us wings to fly high in the sky,
And removes our fear of falling down and die.

It brings us close to our creator,
And teaches us how to save our soul from the traitors,
It purifies our heart and head,
To accept the life's actual facts.

It is an invisible and the most precious wealth,
Which gives us power and immense strength,
No one can steal it, no one can snatch it,
Rather it enhances, while imparting it, bit by bit.

Everything around us imparts us knowledge,
We just need to make ourself positive to get that solace,
So let's submerge ourselves in the ocean of intellect,
Only then we will be able to introspect.

Music

Music is a euphoric melody,
Which takes us away from the mundane fallacy.

It is a universal language of love,
Which is as pure as a dove.

It appeals to our senses,
And fondles our heart crossing all the fences.

It takes us to our own crafted world,
Where our heart can relax , the most.

It reminisces us of the memorable moments,
And flashes before us those special occasions.

It has an ability to take us to the heavenly abode,
What we need is the amalgamation of heart and soul.

It can wipe the tears of a feeble,
And can strengthen him with the vigour of an eagle.

It can arouses the feeling of patriotism and romance,
And even spiritualism, aestheticism and penance.

It expresses our emotions better than our words,
As it directly touches the person’s heart's core.

It soothes the one who is living inside the womb,
And foster the one who is moving towards his doom.

It can cross the border without any endorsement,

As it has its own wings of positivity and reinforcement.

So create your own music for your life,
Which will take you away from all sort of strife.

Silence

Silence speaks louder than words,
It says what words can't express.
It also says what we want to heard,
It also says what is unheard.
It is the reply of many questions,
It is the best solution of many problems.
It makes us more attentive,
As now we can listen to our own heartbeat.
It makes us more responsible,
As it makes the relations more durable.
It makes us more patient,
And enables us to listen others statement.
In the search of silence
We move to distant hills,
As we all are fed up of this key attick world,
Which is adulterating the pure blood of our heart.
So let's try to listen the soulful voices,
Which can take us away from the demonic noises.

Maturity

Maturity is
When we start perceiving God's hints,
And appraising His well-written script.

When we start ignoring the people's mistakes,
And accepting that they have not yet internally awake.

When we stop bothering what others will think,
And start realizing that we all are uniquely distinct.

When the flame of spirituality is kindled within us,
Then we will never have for anyone strong feeling of disgust.

When we start looking at the positive aspect of the people and situation,
It will reduce our stress and will save us from moral degradation.

When we realise our role in this world,
Then we will not be influenced by things which are absurd.

When we understand nothing is everlasting,
Whether it is unpleasant or enchanting.

When we apprehend no one can control our emotions,
As we have the remote control of our passions.

When we perceive that no one can give us happiness,
As it's in our hands to keep ourselves away from scrappiness.

When we conceive that our mind is the superpower,
Which can take us to the success tower.

When we accept that nothing can harm us,
Accept our own weakness and mind's fuss.

When we grasp that every problem comes with a solution,
We just need to have an insight for its execution.

When we discern that argument will worsen the situation,
And we try to do our best for making up and reconciliation.

When we realise silence is the best solution of many disputes,
Which will help us in marching towards progressive pursuits.

When we understand that peace is just inside us,
We don't need to rush to far off places to remove the profane dust.

So let's be mature,
So that we can listen the voice of our soul.

Peace

Peace is what we seek for,
As it gives us an insight to explore ourself more.

We expect this from others,
Forgetting that it is hidden within us.

We move to far off places in its search,
But we find it when our heart and soul gets merge.

It creates a divine aura in our atmosphere,
Which keeps us away from all sort of fear.

It infuses in us the positive spirit,
And embellishes our virtues which we already inherit.

We get it by fusing our heart, mind and soul,
As it armours us with integrity to play our role.

It empowers us to discern other's behaviour,
Which distangles us from filthy maneuver.

It perceives us the actual meaning of life,
As now we are away from the mundane strife.

It gives us wisdom to ruminate about our existence,
As it makes our faith towards our creator persistent.

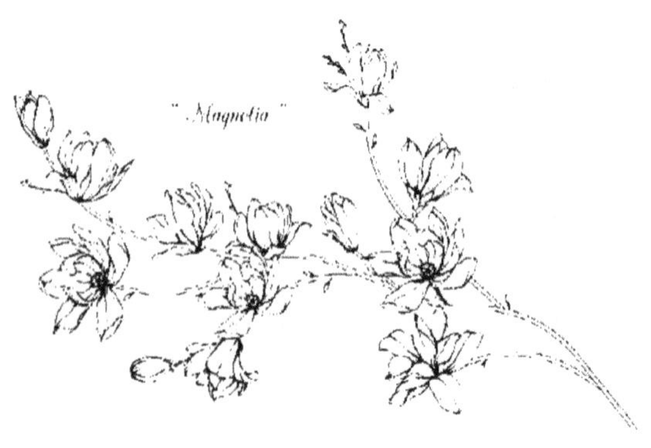

Poems related to our emotions

Success

Success is what we all want,
This is always on demand.

But what is the actual meaning of success,
Let's have a look, how can we get it without having stress.

Success is the feeling of happiness by winning others,
Not the feeling of pleasure by defeating others.

It is the competition with our own self,
By challenging our potentials and do the best.

It is the confidence to face any dare,
And winning it by overcoming our fears.

It can never be measured in monetary terms,
As it is related with contentment and not with the profits of a firm.

It is acquired by those who work consistently,
Forgetting the hardships which one has to face physically and mentally.

But only few can enjoy it for a longer time,
As its vibrations make one feel boastful of his prime.

It is a subjective aspect of our life,
Some get it easily but for some it is a matter of strife.

So if you want to taste the fruit of success,
Pour in your heart and soul to make your path luminous.

Aestheticism

Praising the beautiful creation of God,
With love and with our crafted words,
Brings us close to his abode.
Helps us to know what is good and absurd.

Carnal beauty attracts us the most,
But it's the inner beauty which last us engrossed,
Beauty of thoughts creates an aura around us,
Which is seraphic, divine and free of profane dust.

Beauty of nature is celestial and sublime,

As each flower, tree and creature bloom in its prime,

They are shaded with angelic colours of nature,

And are blessed with their own defensive features.

Beauty of soul makes one eternal,

As the body changes but soul remains vernal,

So let's try to beautify our soul,

Which can enable us to play sincerely our role.

Happiness

Happiness is a state of heart and mind,
Where euphoric secrets of worlds are hide.

Happiness can only be found inside our heart,
And is reflected in our eyes and in our words.

We need an insight to find it out,
As it provides us solace even in the crowd.

It makes us king of our own world,
Where each thought is meticulously pearled.

It enables us to listen to our soul,
And helps us to achieve our goal.

It brings us close to the God,
As pure heart and soul is God's abode.

Don't expect this from others wit,
As no one is worthy of giving you even a bit of it.

Nothing in this world can make you happy,
Accept your sacred heart and mind's positivity.

So nourish yourself with constructive thoughts,
Which can help you to win every race of this earthly road.

Discipline

Discipline is a word which we first heard in our school,

But many a time we have been punished for breaking the rule.

But that punishment teaches us the lesson of discipline,

And makes us a virtuous and patriotic citizen.

Disciplined life is the key to success,

As it helps in evading the life's stress.

Discipline inculcates many moral values in us,

And free our mind and heart from all sort of fuss.

Disciplined mind will take us to the heights,
And well enable you to enjoy the life's delights.

Disciplined heart will enlighten us from the core,
Which will help us to perceive our life's role.

Discipline in relations will never allow us to cross our limits,
As it will always kindle the warmth of relation's spirit.

Soul residing in a disciplined flesh,
Will never make us feel oppressed.

So lets discipline our mind and heart,
And win the battle of this world like a star.

Heart

Every beat of a heart,
Reminds us that we can always restart.

Every ounce of blood it pumps,
Prepares us to face life's strange bumps.

It is full of emotions and feelings,
Which makes us distinct from others in our dealings.

It perceives the unsaid and unheard,
As it is not dependent on sugar coated words.

It includes in it an ocean of blood,

But when it is hurt It pour down the tearful flood.

It is the favourite topic of lyricist, poets and writers,
As they give personal touch to the sentiments of their admirers.

It can make us beautiful or hideous,
As it reflects on our face whatever is hidden in it mysterious.

Whenever we are in trouble,
It guides us and removes the tension like a bubble.

When we love someone it inflates like a balloon,
And love rain stars even without a monsoon.

When it breaks it only pumps the blood,
But is unable to feel and club.

So nourish your heart with love and positivity,
As it will bring in your life auspicious felicity.

Anger

Anger is like a deadly venom,
Which poisons our whole genome.

It spreads in our body so rapidly,
That it affects us from head to toe shabbily.

It has so negative vibrations,
That it paralyses our senses and deteriorate the relations.

It not only perturb the recipient but also the anger creator,
As it serves both of them animosity in a frowzy platter.

It vibrates our heart faster than normal,
And makes us do the actions which are immoral.

It increases the flow of blood in our veins,
And gives our heart and mind, psychic strains.

It is depicted in our harsh words and burning eyes,
Due to which we forget our power to analyse.

It is an outcome of our non-acceptance attitude,
Which always expect others, to change their views.

Once we start accepting and stop expecting
This vengeful toxin will start vanishing.

Booster dose of forgiveness and compassion should be injected in us,
So that we can save ourselves from the viral attack of atrocious fuss.

Fear

We all have some sort of fears,
Some are hidden and some are bare.

Some are dreadful and some are terrible,
Some are perennial and some are ephemeral.

They are like the deepest ditch in the powerful ocean,
Which can disturb the silent water with its violent commotion.

We all hide our fears behind the smiling face,
But when we confront it, all are fakeness is effaced.

We don't want to confront our fears,
But they pursue us in all our worldly spheres.

Suppressing them will only lead to the outburst of burning magma,
Which has been accumulating for years in our plasma.

While shrouding our fears, sometimes we forget our morality,
Which gives birth to the monstrous mentality.

Turning away from the fears is not the solution of any problem,
Facing them and winning them can help us to maintain our decorum.

So, let's face off our deadly fears,
To live our life afresh as a pioneer.

Toughest Battle

Toughest battle in the world,
Is between the head and the heart,
When the heart is swayed by emotions,
The head asks for the reasons.

The heart is easily got tempted,
The head saves us from the tenacious dungeon,
The heart sees the beauty in the people,
The head looks at their intentions.

The heart follows the passion,
Perceives the benevolence and compassion,
Without bothering about right or wrong,
It just follows the rhythm of love.

The head is a stern teacher,
Guides us to follow an ideal path,
Even in the emotional moments,
Doesn't matter how we feel, good or bad.

Brilliant head and generous heart makes us human,

They both are our saviour at some point or other,

So nourish them with positivity and alacrity,

As they would bloom the way they are cultivated.

Disciplined head and heart,

Can win this world without any war,

So resolve this internal battle,

Come out like a shining star and let the world dazzle.

Laugh

Laugh to increase the glow of your face,
It will enhance your beauty and grace,
Laugh to lighten the burden of your heart,
As it will remove the hideous dirt,
Laugh to bring happiness in someone's life,
As it will free them from all sort of strife.
Laugh to thanks God for this beautiful world,
As He's the one who makes this earth whirled.

My tears

My tears are my soul companion,
As they accompany me in life's deep Canyon.

They give vent to my emotions,
Which are as deep as an ocean.

I let them trickle down,
As they remove my worst frowns.

They hide themselves in my sparkling eyes,
Like a beautiful pearl hidden in a Carapace.

They are more expressive than my words,
As they imbibe my feelings in pure hearts.

For some they are just saline water,
But for some they are Adams ale.

They have become an inseparable part of my life,
As they express both my happiness and strife.

Romantic poems

A walk to Remember

Wants to go on a long walk with you,
Where we could enjoy the fascinating view,
Of lush green carpets besides the blue sea,
Welcoming us to indulge in glorious spree.

Holding your hands in mine,
Makes me forget the time,
Looking deep into your eyes,
Makes me satiate and gives me all the replies.

Splashing of water and chirping of birds,
Takes me to the halcyon world,
Where we both will flow with the wind,
And will enjoy our special moments, getting intertwined.

let's make this walk a memorable one,
Let's sing love songs in each others arms,
Let's forget the world for a while,
And let's kill each other with our dazzling smiles.

Ocean

Being submerged in the ocean of your love,
It seems I have my own different world,
Where you and I live in each other's arms,
And enjoying the pleasures of aquatic charm.

It's waves show our variant moods,
Sometimes it shows that we are being wooed,
And sometimes it shows our intense love game,
Which kindles in us an amorous flame.

The counch on its shore,
Shows the fusion of two souls,
Holding in it the beautiful pearl,

To which it doesn't want to unfurl.

I want to be with you in this oceanic atmos,
I feel, I am living in a celestial cosmos,
Here, every creature has become my friend,
And now from here, I don't want to transcend.

Ocean being the symbol of timelessness,
Prepares us to face the ups and downs with fearlessness,
Reminds us that no one can defeat us,
Except our own divine conscious.

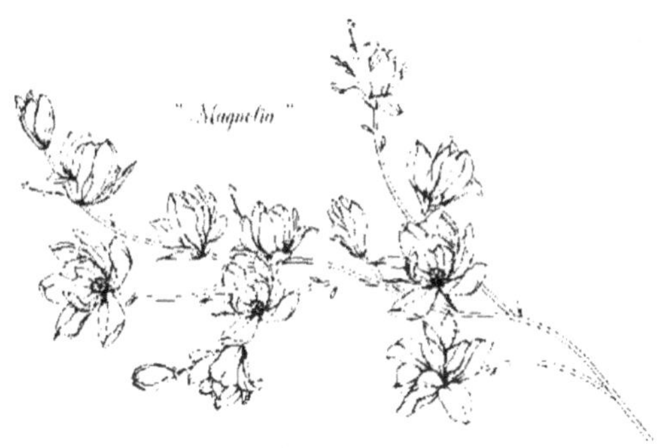

Adventurous journey

Once in search of adventure,
I and my love went deep into the forest,
Leaning in each other's arms,
Intoxicated in love,
We lost our way,
Then begin our adventurous journey,
We hugged each other so tightly,
That we got lip locked,
That my heart could feel his heartbeat,
He could feel my breath,

We were lost in each other's arms,
Watching our love scene,
Even Sun went to take some rest,
After some time,
When we opened our eyes,
Morning Hue was showering its blessings,
The whole nature was fragrant with blossoms,
The birds were singing melodious songs,
Everything was looking fresh and brighten,
The sun was still peeping through dull clouds,
Again holding each other's hands,
We went to find our lost way,
And finally, we came out of the wild forest,
Really it was an amazing journey.

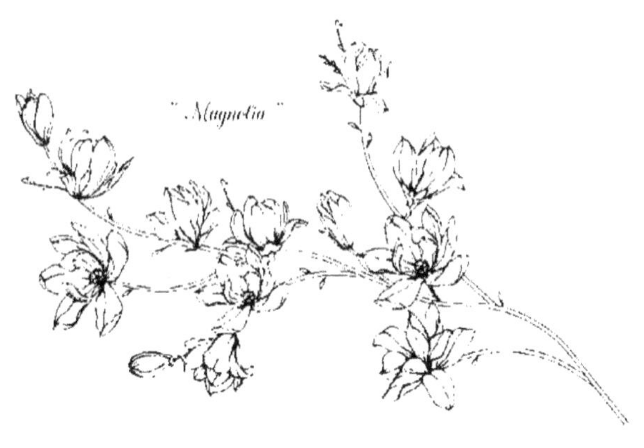

My love

Warmth of your love,
Is so contagious,
That it makes me captive,
Of your body and soul,
It leaves no difference in you end me,
And now I don't want to get free,
Hold me tight in your arms,
And let me smell you with my sense,
Let me imprint my love on you,
And let my body be carved by you,
Let us mingle our souls,
To become one and whole.

My love

My heart blooms like a flower in the
spring,
It started flying even without wings,
When you come close to me,
When you implant your love on me,
I started smelling like you,
Forgetting the difference between me and
you.

Love Song

Ah love!
I can travel on the paper,
To reach your heart,
I can talk to your soul,
With my pure words,
I can take you to the magical world,
Where we both will sing love songs,
We will do whatever we want,
As there would be no one who would haunt,
We will nurture our world with love,
Which will be safeguarded by dove,
No hatred, no violence,
No restrictions, no border and no fence,
For a while air, land and water will become dormant,
As they will cherish our love moments.

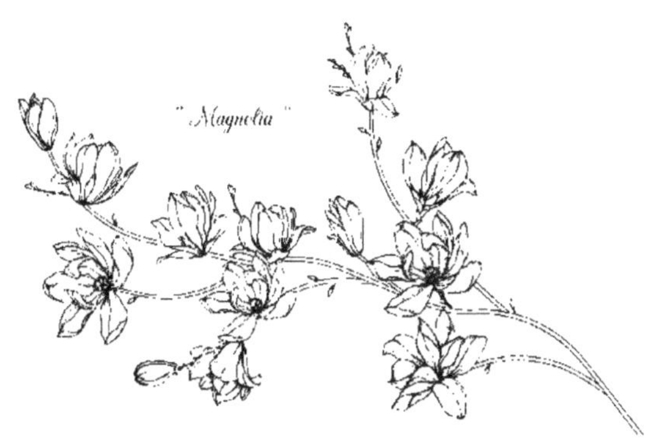

Love In Nature

Peeping through the green leaves,
Red flowers look amazingly sweet,
After meeting their loved ones,
They start blushing at once,
Looking at this enchanting scene,
My heart starts beamed,
I too wanted to be in my lovers arms,
Where I would feel galvanic charm.

Eyes

Oh love!
There's a transparent ocean inside your eyes,
Where I want to take a dive,
And collect the ineffable pearls,
For which I have always yearned,
I will string them together,
To make them look dazzling as heather,
Adorning myself with that pearled string,
Will save me from the Murky sting.

Eternal love

My love for you,
Is like a love of a leaf for a tree,
It falls from it,
It decays,
But is not ready to get separated from it,
So it mingles with the earth,
And start nourishing the same tree,
It's love for the tree is eternal,
And so is mine for you.

Ode to Love

Your love twinkles in my eyes,
Which has brighten my days and nights,
Your fragrance has aromised my life,
And I feel blessed to be your wife,
Wrapping myself in your arms,
Makes me lovealcholic as if I had sauternes,
Loving you and making you happy is my only aim,
And I always want to see both of us smiling in a single frame,
I pray to God to strengthen our bond of love and trust,
Which will never be affected by any furious gust.

Let me

Let me speak out to you my heart,
So that we will become one and never be apart.

Let me dive into the fathom of your eyes,
So that what I want to say, you can analyse.

Let me feel your heartbeat,
So that I could sense what you perceive.

Let me touch your firm skin,
So that I can get rid of harsh grim.

Let me kiss on your forehand,
So that as lovers we can together move ahead.

let me kiss on your lips,
So that I could enjoy the pleasure of your grip.

Let me come close to you,
So that I can shower on you passion of my emotion's hue.

Let me become the indispensable part of your life,
And I assure you, you will feel proud on your wife.

Quotes on Love

Oh Love!

Being drenched in your love,
I forgot myself,
Time passed and,
God knows when you became I,
And I became you.(delete this)

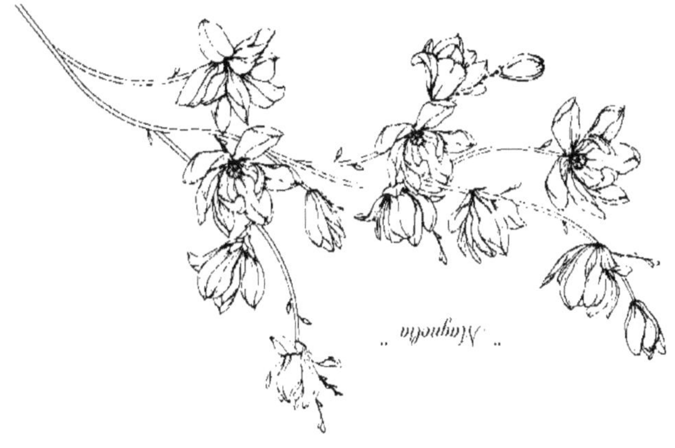

Oh my Lover

"As a sun can't conceal its brightness
As a flower can't conceal its fragrance
As a Peacock can't conceal its alluring plumage
How can I conceal my love for you,
As it's visible in my eyes as a colorful hue,
As it's depicted in my verses as a fascinating view."

Oh my Love

"Suffusing the hue of your love,
On my body and soul,
You made me the captive of your heart,
From which now I don't want to get apart,
So come,
Let's blossom the nature,
With the fragrance of our love."

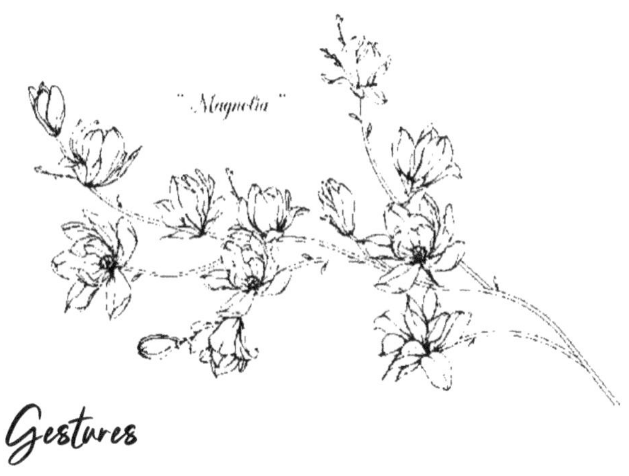

Gestures

We don't need words to voice our emotions,
Our gestures are enough to show our intention,
When the feelings are strong, positive or negative
It reaches its destination on its own,
So don't play with words to delineate yourself,
As our body can pantomimed our vehemence.

Silence

Silence among the nations,
Strengthen the relations,
But
Silence among the relations,
Languish the affinity among the loved ones.

Heart Break

When heart pumps the blood,
But is unable to feel and club.

Peace

Peace can never be found,
Even in the most tranquil mound,
It does not favour an indigent vagabond
And has nothing to do with a supreme crowned,
It resides in a compassionate heart,
Which can find peace,
Even in chaos.

Satisfaction

The satisfaction which we get from doing the work,
Can never be attained by shirking the work,
So
Do your karma,
As you are going to be judged only on that,
Not on others perspective of your life.

Feelings

When your feelings are strong,
It reaches to its destination on its own,
You don't need to say anything,
As your eyes and gestures explicit everything.

Think High

It is impossible to please all,
So
Be true to your conscience,
As here only God resides,
Don't change your principles,
To match with someone's ills,
Rise above the petty trifles,
As it only gives tensions,
Set your goals high,
And work hard to touch the sky.

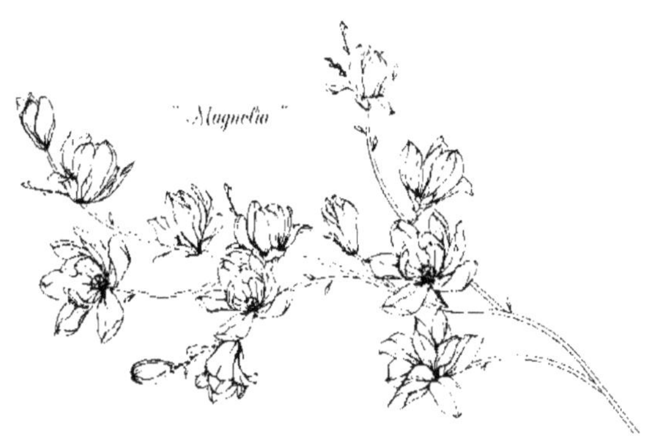

The Crimson sun is peeping,
Through dark clouds,
Suffusing its hue on distant hill,
Brinny water is sparkling in the sea,
Ah love!
Flabbergasted by this charismatic scene,
I yearn to be in your arms to sheen.

When negativity hovers around me,
Like bees dance around the flowers in glee
Then you come as an apiarist,
And transmute that animosity,
Into sweet honey of fidelity.

Teacher's Proposal

After teaching you loveology,
I have deduced that you are,
Awesome in ecology,
Majestic in cuddology,
Stupefying in kissology,
But I want to ask you
Will you be my passionate student in liviology,

Passionate Poems

Superpower Mind

Mind is our superpower,
Which can even bring celestial shower,

It is a creator,
It is a destroyer,

It makes us glad,
It makes us sad,

It makes us liberate,
So that proficiency could invigorate.

It makes us strong,
And empower us to stand against the wrong.

It has the power to make us rule,
It has the power to enslave us too.

It can reveal the hidden truths of life,
And can save us from the world's strife.

It makes us aware of our potentials,
And enables us to ratify which is essential.

So, if we can control our minds,
Nothing can stop us from being shined.

let yourself to live

Let the zypher to stroke your hair,
Let the raindrops to fall on your soft cheeks,
Let the sunrise to shine on you,
Let the nature to nurture you,
let the shackles of restrictions be broken,
let yourself listen to your heart,
Let yourself to grow from within,
Let yourself to live.

Dreams

Dreams seen with open eyes,
Will never let you sleep at night.

Move forward to achieve your goal,
So that you will always be extolled.

Chase the dreams with your head and heart,
So that targets could be hit by your assiduous dart.

But don't pursue your dreams frantically,
Else you will dwindle drastically.

Enjoy the journey of accomplishing your dreams,
As it will teach you how to convert secrets of life's stream.

Hard work is the key to success,
Which you can get at any age, I guess.

Age is just a reminder,
That you are still a pathfinder.

Age can make you fumble,
But can never make your dreams crumble.

So forget the age,
And be a young maze.

Life Changing Decision

Two roads diverged in a yellow wood,
I didn't know what to choose,

One was rough and one was smooth,
But both took to the different routes,

Both were alluring me to their side,
And I got confused in choosing the right,

With a heavy heart, I choose the one,
In which I thought I could run,

It had pebbles and hurdles,
But with God's grace I was able to overcome,

I don't know whether my decision was right or wrong,
But it was because of that only, today I could sing a success song.

Feelings

Feelings for someone are like the bubbles,
If handled with love and care,
Will surely shower fragrant flowers,
Which will make our lives like our heavenly bower,
Else
It will burst out,
Leaving behind it's small fragments,
Which will be sans warmth and a harrowing torment

Words and Heart

Kind words,
Enliven the heart,
Bitter words,
Shatter the heart,
But unsaid words,
Loiter the heart,
And leads to ambiguity,
So speak up whatever is in your heart,
And resolve the dilemma.

My Mood Swings

When I am happy,

My heart feels like a valley of flowers,

Which spreads its fragrance,

And blooms everyone's heart,

But sometimes those flowers transmute into thorns of desert,

Which are sans warmth and sans love,

And it seems its thorns are pricking my own wounds,

And torturing me with rumbling growls,

So

Being in a state of ecstasy or in a gloom is in our own hands,

When we are happy, the whole world sparkles with an optimistic view,

But when we are sad the whole world seems to be shrouded with a pessimistic hue.

Today's youth

Today's youth is the future of this world,
Who has magnanimous energy and vigorous blood.

He has rational and scientific aptitude,
Which helps him to explore the hidden secrets of our earth.

He has not only excavated the terrain,
But with his flabbergasted potential has reached the empyrean.

He has become a friend of marine and wild creatures,
Who help him to click their fabulous pictures.

Today's youth doesn't believe in spiritual rituals, as he is busy in his factual coherence.

But unfortunately

Rational thinking has reduced the man to a robot,

Which can do all the functions but is sans emotions.

Today's youth is blindly moving on, to win the world.

Forgetting the key of success, that is their pure heart.

Alas!

God has created a beautiful creature called man,

But this creature has been brutally murdered by his own scientific clan.

Hope!

What we need today is the amalgamation of head and heart,

Only this could save us from this rancorous world.

Life

Life is what you make it,
God help those who deserve it,
Help yourself to set your goals,
Work hard to put in it your soul,
Don't rely on others,
As you have the fire,
Let that fire to ignite your passion,
Don't transmute towards the latest fashion,
Burn yourself today,
To enjoy the warmth tomorrow,
Raise your heart and mind,
Don't let it sway with the wind,
No one can change us,
Without our willingness,
Whatever we sow,
The same we reap,
Sow the seeds of hope,
It will give you a very healthy crop,
Enjoy the life but don't forget,
We have it just for once,
So make it fruitful for everyone.

Intensity of love

Can't you see the intensity of your love in my eyes?

Can't you hear the echo of my heartbeat?

Can't you utter what I want to listen?

Can't you pierce through my soul and coalesce in me?

If you can't perceive my inking even now,

Then tell me what should I do,

To tell what you are for me?

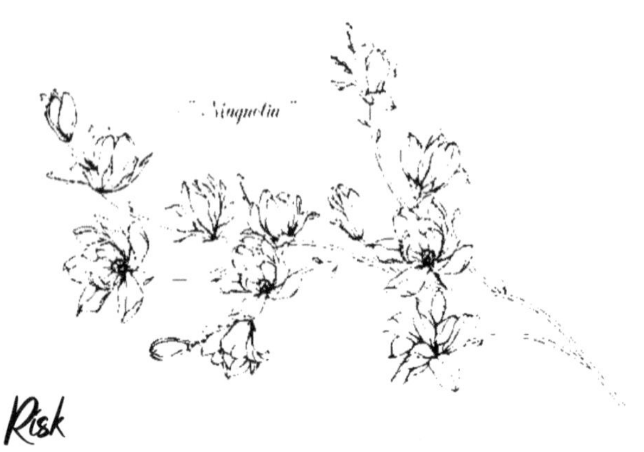

Risk

Risk is to be taken,
If soul is to be awaken,
Those who smilingly face the hurdles,
Don't consider anything as a burden,
They follow the path of success,
And shine like a fluoresce,
So don't hesitate to take a risk,
And let your life move at a brisk.

Optimistic poems

Art of living

Life is a web of thorns and flowers,
But only a hard worker can get success in its every path.

Life is a short period between birth and death,
So, finish all your responsibilities before leaving this world.

Whenever you are in trouble listen to your heart,
As it is the only place free from world's materialistic dirt.

Turn the wheel of your life on the path of truth and love,
And remove the word hatred from everybody's heart.

Leave behind the marks of your glory on everybody's mind,
So that you will live alive even when you might have died.

For you people

Oh! man why are you sleeping?
See Sun has risen with its bright light,
Every creature is waiting for your awakening,
So wake up and remove the darkness from your eyes.

Oh! man why are you so sad?
Listen the voices of the creatures of nature,
who are playing and looking very glad,
So you too cheer up and enjoy the life's real treasure.

Oh man! why are you fighting?
Please don't harm the beautiful nature created by God,
Let them enjoy the beauty of nature who are enjoying,
So stop fighting and spread the flowers of love in your world.

If you have

If you have a heart,
Try to remove the word hatred from this world,
Spread the flowers of love,
It will make you feel like a dove.

If you have eyes,
Try to see the beauty even in the mice,
Admire the beautiful creation of God,
It will make you feel richest of all.

If you have hands,
Try to cultivate even the barren land,
Sow the seeds of hope,
It will give you a very healthy crop.

If you have ears,
Try to listen the sobs of poor,
Embrace them and wipe off their tears,
It will give you a heartly pleasure.

Failure To Success

Failure is the first step towards the success,
As it is an inspiration to do the best.

Failure enlightens the man's internal spirit,
And enables him to use his power and
wit.

Failure awakens the man from deadly sleep,
And helps him to fulfill all his dreams.

Failure teaches the man the value of time,
And makes him punctual and wise.

Failure arouses the feeling of competition,
As it is the key to reach the destination.

Failure helps the man to know the realities of life,

And tells him the difference between the wrong and the right.

Today's failure is an indication of tomorrow's victory,

So work hard to get this precious ivory.

Determination

It is difficult to part away from the things,
With which our heart has already clinged.

We make them an important part of our life,
And leaving them becomes a sort of strife.

But if we know that temporary pleasure,
Is going to take away from, our real treasure,

Then it's better to make ourself firm,
So that in future we don't have to squirm.

Really it's better to maintain a distance from those things,
Which can use against us it's venomous sting.

And it's really better to bear the transitory pain,
Than to hear the perpetual heart's wail.

But if we want to have a bright future,
We have to keep ourselves away from the deadly tumour.

Hope

Hope can enlighten the dead soul,
Which can save us from the unbearable loss.

Hope spreads the flowers of positivity in our ambience,
Whose fragrance make our life vibrant and marvelous.

Hope is an Oasis in the dry desert of our life,
Which can help us to quench our life's essence.

Hope is like a warm covering given to the flame of earthen lamp,

Which is fluttering due to the gust of humanities vamp.

Hope is a silver lining in this gloomy sky,

Which is surviving us and encouraging us that we can still fly high.

Hope can make us fulfil our dreams,

And can help us to proceed our realms.

Hope can make all good things possible,

And can help us to come out of the deadly torment.

Hope is the only treatment in this sick world,

Which can save us from the monster of this suicidal predicament.

Expectations versus Acceptance

Expectations leads to frustrations,
Amongst relations,
Acceptance leads to solace,
Which ascends the relation's grace
So don't expect anything from anyone,
As they are not worthy of giving you even a bit,
Accept the things and people as they are,
As it will increase your acceptance bar,
And will help you forget the bitter scars.

Spring

Spring is the season of regeneration,
Fills the atmos with beautification,
Scented the flowers with aromatic hue,
And dazzles our eyes with panoramic view.

It is the season of revival for everyone,
When all are ready to blossom in Sun,
When the cool breeze soothes our heart,
And enlightens in us for life, a new spark.

It's a season of hope and positivity,
Which enables us to explore our creativity,
It gives birth to many poets, lyricists and writers,

Who, with their writings, win the heart of their admirers.

It is a season of lovers,
Who enjoy in the arms of each others,
Their hearts blossom with love,
And they want to fly in the sky like a dove.

It is a season of optimism and dreams,
Which gives us a chance to redeem,
It shows the never-ending circle of time,
And shows us the short duration of every clime.

So, let's enjoy the beauty of every season,
As God has created every season with a reason,
And gives a message that life is too short,
So, live every moment with memorable shots.

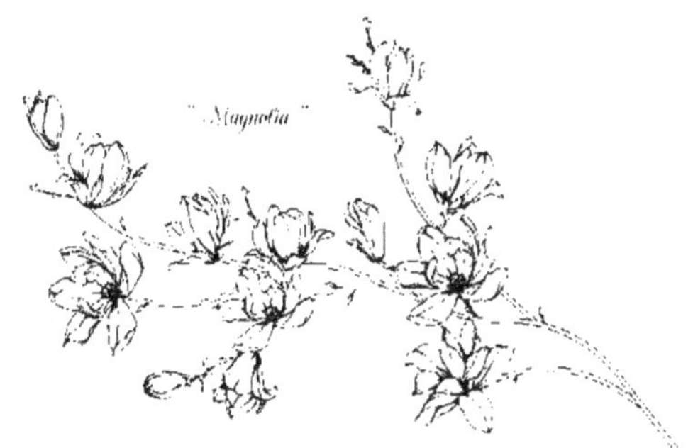

Forgive and Forget

These 2 FS can change our life,
And will make it benign and divine,
Let's adopt these two doctrines,
It will avert us from the venomous toxins.

Let's forgive the one who does wrong to us,
It will keep us away from the absurd fuss,
It will save our positive energy,
And will make us do our actions disciplinary.

Forgiveness will bring us close to our creator,
And will empower us with the miraculous power,
To see the goodness in all his animates,
And making their life brilliantly luminous.

But let's not forget the one who stands by us in the toughest time,

As they are the one who help us to bear all the climes,

They're like the angels of God,

Who rescue us from the profane, devious plot.

Let's not forget to help them when they are in need,

As time teaches everyone, how to pull out the weeds,

So let's complete our karma chakra in this world,

So that we don't have to pay back with interest in next birth.

So forgive the sinners,

For your life to be healthier,

And enshrine the holy spirits,

Who shower astounding blessings on us without any limit.

Poems related to poetry

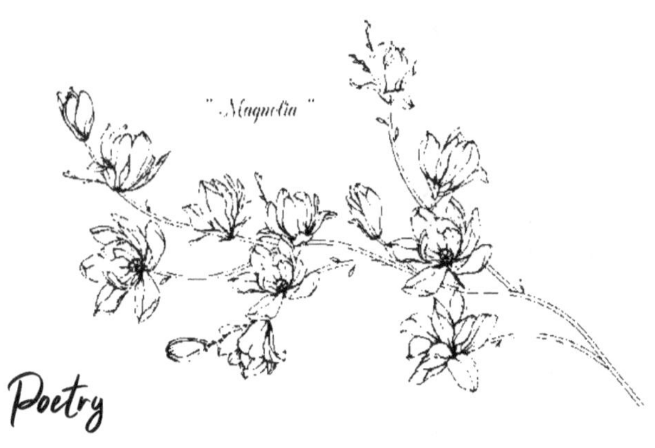

Poetry

Words jiggle in my mind,
Like a wind chime.
Words struck my heart,
As if I have left something unheard.
Till the time I don't string the words together,
It seems to me as if I have lost my feathers.
Poetry gives me a magical power,
And it takes me to the fancy's highest tower.
Poetry has become an indispensable part of my life,
As it soothes my heart and free me from all sort of strife.
Poetry brings a smile on my face,
As it's like the idyllic flowers in an elegant vase.

Power of words

Playing with words is an art,
Those who know this can win anyone's heart.

One can do miracle with the words,
As they have the power to touch one's soul.

Words have the power to enslave others,
As they can directly touch one's emotions.

Words can make us visualise the scenes,
As they appeal through all our senses.

Words can make the history alive,
As they preserve its rich heritage and culture.

Words can help us to foresee the future,
As they give us an insight into world's hidden treasure.

Words have their own vibrations,
Which can mould once perspective towards any situation

Arrows of words can slaughter one so painfully,
That even medicines fail to work on them truly.

Invigorating words can bring spring in the winters,
And can bloom fresh flowers, overcoming all the hindrance.

So pick your words prudently from your lexicon,
As they leave a long-lasting impact on one's mind.

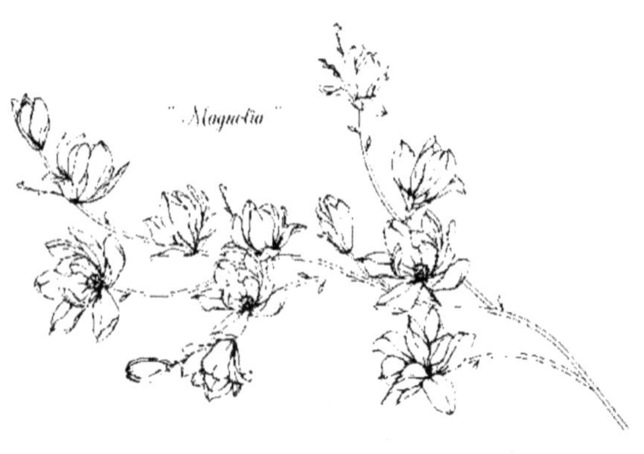

Who is a Poet?

Poet is the one,

Who can fly with the wings of imagination,

Who can sing melodies without any musician,

Who can delineate a portrait without any actual impression

Who can hear the unheard voices in the sheer silence,

Who can perceive the unseen,

Who can fondle the delicate symphonies,

Who can aromised his verses,

Who writes with his empathetic heart,

Which can assuage any torment,

And can also act like a sharp dart.

If poetry was a person!

If poetry was a person,
I would become its soul,
I would make it alive,
By pouring in it feelings,
So whosoever will read it,
Will feel as if
Each word is whispering something in his ears,
Each word is touching his heart,
Each word is delineating a new scenery,
Each word is tangling his palate,
Each word is stroking his skin,
Finally by merging myself in those words,
We both would become eternal.

Aesthetic Poetry

Playing with words,

And wreathing them,

In the beautiful metrical strings,

Gives me my own magical wings,

Using which I fly in the utopian world,

Where everyone is busy in making their strings pearled,

Spellbound by their creations,

I fell as if I have dived in dilettante's ocean,

Where everything is sublime in nature,

And that reminds me of our world's creator,

Wants to live in this cosmo's forever,

Where I would remain busy in my own endeavour.

Feel the Poetry

Not all poems are meant to be read,
Some are meant to be felt,
With a pure heart,
Some are meant to be visualised,
With closed eyes,
Some are meant to be heard,
Like the warbling of the bird,
Some are meant to be tasted,
With love buds,
Really
Not all poems are meant to be read.

Biography of a Paper

I am a paper,
Canvas of a poet,
Where he paints his emotions,
In a metrical, embellishing and euphonious way,
Using different colours gifted by life,
He paints his soul and heart on me,
And I express everything who gazed at me.

My love

My poetry sails,
From my heart,
Reaches yours,
Overcoming all storms.

An ode to Poetry

Poetry is my first love and now my life,
It gives me refuge when I feel it's difficult to survive.

It takes me to the world of imagination,
Where from everything I get emancipation.

I pour out my heart in my poetry,
Which relieves me of stress and anxiety.

It expresses my emotions in rhythmic strings,
And brings in my life a blossoming spring.

It has given me wings to fly in the sky,
Now I can even play with clouds while flying high.

It comes to me so spontaneously and naturally,
That now I can build my own creative world architecturally.

It has given me an opportunity to dive in my own heart,
And has helped me in collecting the revered pearls.

Sometimes I feel it has done on me a magic spell,
Which has helped me a lot in excelling myself.

It has discovered a new person in me,
Who has now become humanity's devotee.

It has bring me close to my own soul,
Which is helping me a lot in achieving life's goal.

I can spend my whole day playing with words,
As it acts as a stimulant for my edgy nerves.

I always wanted to be in this utopian world,
Where I could enjoy the mystical melodies undisturbed.

Spiritual Poems

Spiritualism

Spiritualism is the connection of soul with almighty,
And this acquaintance enables one to shine brightly.

It permeates us with divine brilliance,
And suffuse us with exquisite resilience.

It always shows us the right path even in the darkest night,
As it is directly linked with our soul, which act as it's valiant knight.

It arouses in us the feeling of affinity for other souls,
Which shows that we all are stringed together with same pearls.

These are the pearls of love for humanity,
Adorning which, will enhance our inner beauty.

It gives us an insight to know ourselves in a better way,

And awakens us from the deadly slumber of moral decay.

It armours us to face the challenges of life with positive spirit,

And it embellishes us with dynamic power and scintillating wit.

It teaches us the role of karmas in our life,

Which no one can evade except the celestial light.

It brings us close to our rich heritage and culture

And disciplined us to become the life's plunger.

It infuses in us the acceptance power,

And exhilarates us in ethereal bower.

So it brings us close to our creator,

And reveals us the hidden secrets of our endeavour.

Magical karmas

Hey man!
Why are you wondering here and there,
When the whole world is inside you.

Why are you carrying holy water from far off places,
When the tap water can become more pious with your prayers.

Why are you going for pilgrimage,
When your own home can become a shrine if you chant God's name.

Why are you collecting Prasad from religious places,
When the food cooked with love can do miracles.

Why are you taking a dip in holy water,
As no holy water that can wash your sins.

It is only sterling karmas,
Thar can save you from rancorous world.

Modern version:

Hey dude,

Why are you clicking selfies,

As you don't need to please yourself.

Why are you photoshopping your pics and to please whom,

Because who loves you, don't bother how you look,

And those who don't will never bother about your flaunts.

Why are you uploading your family trips on social media,

As noone is interested in searching you about in Wikipedia.

We are the perfect creation of God,

We can use our senses in any way we want.

As our eyes can click the luminous photos and delete the gloomy,

As our mind can store the relevant and remove the irrelevant ideas,

As our ears can listen the best and unheard the worst,

As our tongue can make us a Saint or a devil,

As our touch can make others tranquilise or exasperate,

So do your charismatic karma with your magical powers,

And make this place a halcyon world.

Karmic Accounts

Whatever we do we are accountable for that,
Our every deed is kept in a record.

Whatever happens is the result of our actions,
No one can evade its counter reactions.

Every thought we create has its own vibrations,
Which can bring us damnation or salvation.

He has the balance sheet of our anathema and blessings,
So He can give and snatch whatever we are possessing.

Whoever enjoys the richest of this earth,

Has actually done something marvellous in his previous birth.

Benediction and malediction of previous birth can have an impact on our life,

But our today's karmas can bring misery and can also free us from strife.

So let's not bother about other's actions,

As we are going to be judged on our reactions.

Our karma's follow us till the eternity,

So let's do our actions with sincere dignity.

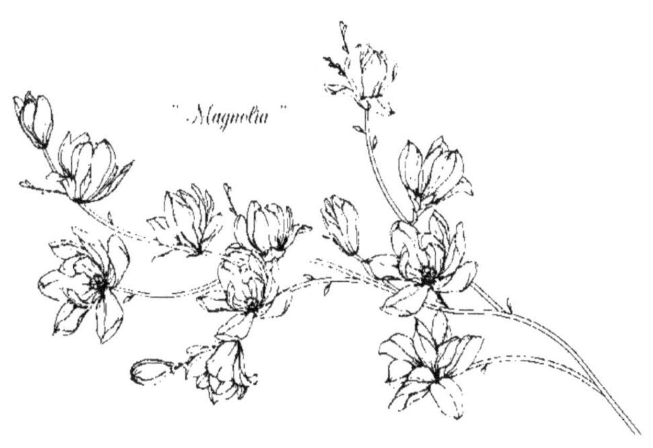

He - The Great

He is with me in my days,
He is with me in my dreams,
He is with me in my joys,
He is with me in my sorrows,
He is everywhere,
He is in everything,
He observes my every deed,
And rewards me accordingly,
He teaches me the real meaning of life,
It's bringing joy in His people's life,
He is the one who is our creator,
He is the one who is our nurturer,
He is the one who allow us to live on His earth,
By sending his messengers who makes our life worth,
If we will not follow his simple rules,
He will kick us out of his abode,
So be thankful to Him for his benevolence,
As he is the one who can save us from all sort of demolishment.

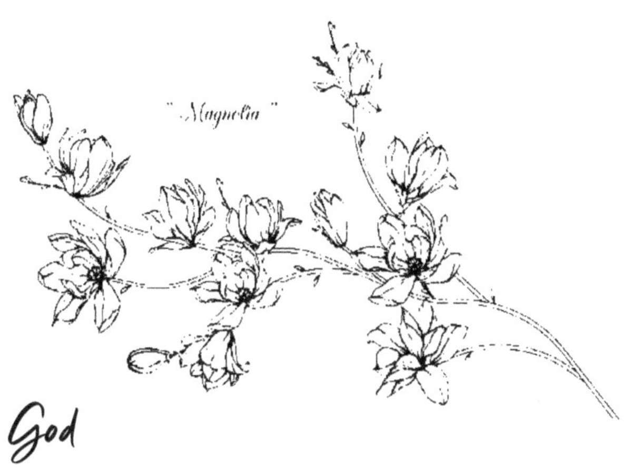

God

Oh Lord!
Your presence in me,
Is like a full moon in Glee,
You have brightened my darkest nights,
Which now sparkles in your gleaming light,
Your reflection is visible in my life,
As it is now free from all sort of strife,
Thank you for always showering your blessings,
As it has made my life dazzling and satiating.

Nature

Nature is an abode of the supreme power,
Blessed are those who gets a chance to live in his Bower.

Everything in the nature teaches us something,
Realizing which, our imagination gets its wings.

Rivers instructs us never to stop,
As behind every hurdle there is a hope.

Mountains guide us to be firm,
But with changing time many things have to be learnt.

Wind directs us to follow our aim,
Overcoming all obstacles, we have to win the life's game.

Sand polishes us to transform ourselves according to the age,
So that we can face all troubles like a young mage.

Trees advise us to be strong and blossoming,
So that, to the humanity we could prove to be promising.

Sky instructs us to be limitless,
So, we should use our potentials to taste the fruit of success.

Sun prepares us to be disciplined and benefactor,
To shine, we have to burn ourself in drudgeries reactor.

Moon is a symbol of ethnic beauty and pacification,
And teaches us the value of tranquillity and integration.

Stars tell us to be consistent in our work,
Without expecting from anyone any sort of perk.

Every creator illustrates us the dignity of labour,
And shows that hard work is the key to success and not anyone's favour.

So, everything in nature is suffusing us with virtues,
Then why we humans are behaving like a materialistic statue?

Blessings

Blessings have miraculous potency,
To save us from all sort of fallacy.

Blessings can regenerate our potentials,
And in life's every aspect acts as a credential.

Blessings come to our rescue when we are in trouble,
And supports us at every point and never let us crumble.

Blessings can reduce the painful impact of our previous birth,
And it's the only way we can save ourself from the vengeful curse.

Blessings let us enjoy each and every phase of life
And takes us out of the serpentine waves of strife.

Blessings are like the lighthouse for a lost sailor,

By showing him the brightest path, acts as his saviour.

Blessings can do the wonders in our life,
As it brings the divine shower of happiness and delight.

Blessings can make us humble and gracious,
And enables us to bring the holy shower on others.

Blessing can make us win anyone's heart,
As they can kindle in others compassionate spark.

So let's earn the blessings as much as we can,
As they have the power to execute our positive plans.

Poems related to relations

Soulful Relations

Beautiful relations with some beautiful souls,
Are closest to our heart's core.
Spending time with them,
Is like investing in a precious gem.
They make us laugh, they make us weep,
That's why our relation with them is so unique,
They always think good for us,
As their heart is free of materialistic dirt,
Our well-being is their top most priority,
Which shows their level of maturity,
I pray to God to keep our bond stronger,
So that we could make this relation memorable.

Special One

People may come people may go,
But only few stay in our heart to glow,
We share a unique bond of trust with them,
Which cannot be seen but can only be felt.

Some invisible force bring us close,
And give us time to share a lot,
The moments spent together are the best,
As they make us feel better than the rest.

They are actually the special ones,
With whom we always want to be in touch.
I wish happiness and success for their life,
And may they always remain away from all sort of strife.

Special Souls

Few souls enter in our life to illuminate it,
And their very existence,
Makes us aware of so many things,
About our lives and about this world.

We have a special bond with them,
Which no one can understand,
It is so unique that it demands nothing,
But is ready to sacrifice everything.

May be they enter in our life for short period,
But they bloom it with fragrant hues,
Which makes it vibrant and radiant,
That invigorate us to live with effervescence .

They always remain close to our heart,
May be actually they are too far,
We may not be in contact,
But their well being will always be our concern.

Thank you God for sending them in our lives,
As they are special and make us feel the same.

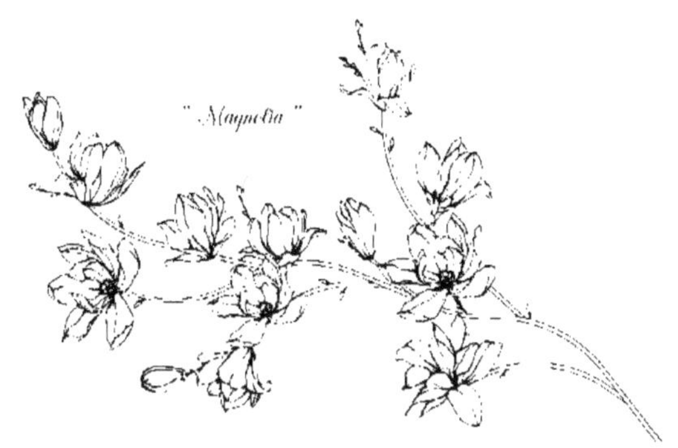

Friendship

Friendship based on conditions,
Is sans feelings and emotions,
As it will be like a cheap bargain,
Which is meant only for personal gain.

Friendship based on mutual respect and trust,
Can easily bear any powerful gust,
So respect that bond,
Which has bought you close.

Don't put restrictions,
As it will disgrace the relation,
So let others to grow,
Your support will help them achieve their goal.

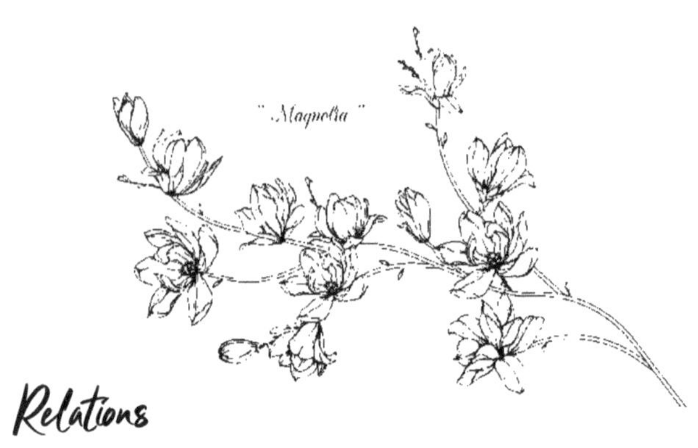

Relations

Beautiful relations with beautiful people,
Make our life humble and stable.

In true relations we don't demand anything,
As we accept each other in every situation.

We support each other through thick and thin,
As being linked with souls we have nothing to do with the skin.

Relation with our soul,
Can help us to play perfectly our life's role.

Relation with the Highest Power,
Can help us to take some relief in His bower.

Relations based on conditions does not last long,

As they are sans feelings and sans emotions.

Relations are like the flowers of love stringed together,

Whose fragrance sparkles our life forever.

Trust and respect are the foundation of any relation,

On which we can build our Empyreal mansion.

True relations does not demand any explanation,

As they believe in making up and reconciliation.

True relations bring a celestial aura in our life,

And empower us to overcome earthly hurdles with a smile.

Dominance has no place in true relations,

As it can lead to misunderstanding and frustration.

In true relations we adore each other's dignity,

Which enhance our love, integrity and felicity.

So let's fortify our relations with fidelity and affection,

Which will vitalise our honest and ethical connection.

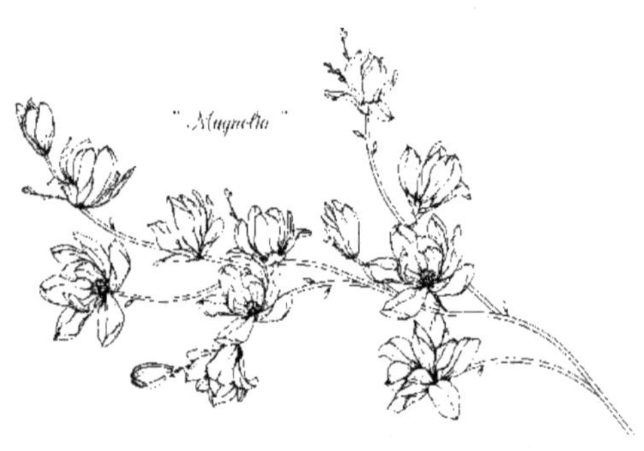

Home

Home is home,
If there is mom,
Her aura brightens our life,
And we forget the worldly strife,
Her lap is the world's best mattress,
Which magically relieves our stress,
She is an angelic architect,
Who can make a home perfect.
Anywhere from a scratch,
Which could be made of cement or thatch,
Smile of her face is so contagious,
Which makes our home super gracious,
She is the heart and soul of our home,
Who's delineation we can never search from Chrome.
Love you mom.

Family- A String of Pearls

Family is a string of pearls,
Woven in the threads of love and trust.

Strength of this string depends,
On the fidelity among the relations.

Each and every pearl has its own identity,
So nothing should be done to harm its serenity.

The shine of the pearls are enhanced with understanding,
Which makes the string look more enchanting.

If the string is embellished with positivity,
It can bring in the life of pearls an immense felicity.

Pearls should not be so tightly packed,
That it does not get enough space and clacked.

Pearls should also not be loosely tied,
That the gap between their hearts become wide.

So string of pearls should be designed and styled in such a way,
That it becomes fragrant like the fresh flowers of a bouquet.

Memorable Memories

I would rather weave a poem,
With your left-over memories,
Than trickling the tears,
While remembering you,
I don't want to disgrace,
The bond we share,
As its uniqueness,
Does not demand anything,
It just spread happiness,
Among the others,
It speaks in volumes,
Without uttering even a word,
It makes me croon the songs,
Which I have always longed,
It brings a smile on my face,
It has gleamed my nights and days,
It has some magical vibrations,
Which makes me aware of your well-being,
So it doesn't matter,
You are here or far apart,
Your memories will always be close to my heart.

Miscellaneous

City life

City life has snatched the fragrance of our soil,
Which has actually made our earth to boil.
Skyscrapers have taken away our blue sky,
Which is just an illusion where no one can fly.
Black air has taken the place of fresh one,
Whose density can even shadowed our bright Sun.
Big craters filled with water has lost its purity,
And people in cities have no decent futurity.
Moving back to our green lands,
Is the last option left in the man's hand,
So nurture your green world with compassion
And enjoy the natures shower of love and passion.

Raindrops are like the pearls from heaven,
They quench the thirst of every raven.

It revamps the nature's health,
And transmute it into gracious wealth.

It is a nature's own personal cleanser,
Which helps to cool down its temper.

It spreads the hue of love in the air,
And blooms every heart and flower with care.

It inspires the people to write,
And enables them to make their literature alive.

It brings the nature with preeminent beauty,
And sways us far from our life's somber reality.

So let these sprinklers to fall on your carcass,
And let them emancipate you from your inner darkness.

Woman- The Creator Of The World

Woman is the creator of this world,
So her name comes even before God.

She is blessed with a divine power,
Of giving birth to our new flower.

She is an idol of love and sacrifice,
So she has a respectable image in everybody's eyes.

She has inspired the people to write,
And is responsible for making the literature alive.

Her beauty is a mystery for this world,
Which has created many histories and cultures.

Laying the strong foundation of love in this world,
Woman has shown this chaotic world a ray of hope.

An embodiment of intellect, sacrifice, strength and love,

Woman has a power to make this place, a better world.

Today woman is touching the sky of success,

So adore her for her work and not for her sex.

To say more about a woman,

Is like to show a candle to the Sun.

Soldiers

Soldiers are the real heroes of the nation,
Who are worthy of divine salvation.

They fight for the honour of their country,
And bear each bruise and lesion numbly.

The dignity of a soldier can't be compared to anyone,
As their valour makes them eternal like a Sun.

From the training to the battlefield, they show their patience,

So we rever them as an idol of obeisance and deference.

They are the lionhearted sons of the motherland,
Who sincerely follow their seniors' command.

They have muscles of iron and nerves of steel,
Which infuse in them patriotic and fervent zeal.

They can live in extreme hot and cold weather,
Which shows that they have the ability to turn the zephyr.

Their festivals, functions and special occasions,
Are all sacrificed for their earnestness and passion.

Their homecoming is waited by their families,
But when their corpse came it rebut their fallacies.

They Defend the borders of their country dauntlessly,

Facing challenges coming their way relentlessly.

They are actually angels in disguise,
Who are born to save others from demise.

So salute these champions who bring happiness in our lives,
By sacrificing their blissful moments of delights.

Power of time

Time has a supernatural power,
If you give it to an unknown,
You will win his heart,
But
If you don't it give it to your loved ones,
Gradually they will move apart,
To help someone with money can be paid back,
But golden moments spent with someone can never come back.
Time is the best gift which you can give to your loved ones,
As it's the one which they can never buy from anywhere else.
Respect and care the ones who spent their precious time to make your moments memorable,
As lots of sacrifices may have been made to make those moments favourable.
So don't avoid those who love you from the core of their heart,
As they are the one who stands by you in all your times.

Flowers

Aromising the nature with its fragrant hues,
Changing the colour of sky from its usual blue,

The purest thing to offer the deities,
Which is sublime and has no artificiality.

Blooming the heart of lovers with delightful pleasure,
Realising them the importance of love which lasts forever.

Bringing the radiant smile on our face,
Which enhance our own beauty and grace.

Sparkling our eyes with dazzling light,
Which makes our aura intensely bright.

The fresh festoons make our celebrations divine,
As their ambrosial fragrance makes everything benign.

Bees suck juices from them,
And while making honey they become overwhelm.

They are the love beds of many small creatures,
Who spent on them their moments of leisure.

These are our lovely flowers,
Who are imbibed with magical superpowers.

Writing about them takes me to a redolent excursion,
Where I have found my own new anthophile version.

My Eyes

My eyes are the reflection of my heart,
They dazzle the others with my luminous spark.

They express what my lips deny,
As they always utter the truth and never live.

They explicit my sorrows and my joys,
As they say everything without making any noise.

They can attract anyone towards it,
As they have the power to slay them bit by bit.

They can control others with their dominance,
For which they are already prominent.

They can show the anger with their burning black balls,
Which can aggravate any belligerent brawl.

They can express love with its enchanting grace,
And can cast a magical spell with its warm embrace.

They can hide the fear in its almond shells,
Where anyone with vibrant heart can dwell.

They give vent to my deep emotions,
Which are interwoven with soulful relations.

They hide in them my sparkling tears,
Which are as pure as my divine prayers.

They are like a mirror to my heart and soul,
But only few can penetrate into it, to extol.

About the Poet

Here, we are going to introduce you to a budding poet Reyansh Mahajan of 9 years. He is very smart and intelligent. He loves to watch horror and adventurous movies. And after watching movies, he starts writing his own stories. He is a good writer. He loves to write poems based on his own experiences and the ideas which he gets from the movies.

So, get ready to enjoy the roller coaster drive,
With the blossoming poet and his rhymes.

School

Schools are very important for us,
We play games even in our school bus.

School days are the best days,
Here secretly, we eat a packet of lays.

In the school, we do a lot of fun,
We play together when our work is done.

We play many games like cricket and football,
We also celebrate many festivals in our school hall.

In the school, we also learn dance and skates,
But we do it, in our style and in our ways.

Teachers make our studies easy,
They make us active when we feel lazy.

Now sitting at Home, I miss my school days,
In which we solve many interesting maze.

Due to lockdown, we cannot go to school,
And I really miss my school's swimming pool.

Now I am really fed up in my home,
Wants to go to school, wearing my school uniform.

I pray to God to open my school,
For this, I can follow even strict school rules.

Teacher

Teachers are like an Angel and phoenix,
Because they give us imaginary wings.

They are like our mother and father,
With their guidance we can find the life's treasure.

Sometimes they scold, sometimes they love,
But their concern for us is as pure as a dove.

Teachers are very motivating,
They do everything to make us creative.

They play a key role in our life,
As they enable us to face bravely life's strives.

They empower us to achieve our goals,
Which give satisfaction and happiness to our soul.

So, we should always respect our teachers,
As they make us God's unique creature.

Books

Books are very important for us,
I read my books even in my school bus.

Books give us a lot of knowledge,
So we should read it, irrespective of our age.

Books play a key role in our studies,
So I read my books with my buddies.

Books make us wise and kind,
And they also help us to sharp our mind.

We always learn something from every book,
So we should never judge a book from its
outlook.

Books are our best friends,
So we should read a book till the end.

Friends

Friends are sweeter than our relatives,
And in each other's company, we feel motivated.

We can share anything with our friends,
Like our favourite food and special secrets.

In the company of good friends, we can achieve anything,
But without friends, the world seems nothing.

True friends never cheat and lie,
But sometimes, we fight on useless things, but I don't know why?

I know we all have some special friends,
And for me they will be special till the end.

Holidays

Holidays are the best days,
We do everything in our ways.

No homework and no studies,
In every holiday, I play with my buddies.

In holidays, I do everything,
And I feel like I'm flying with my wings.

In holidays we do not get up early morning,
No one teaches and nobody gives us warning.

No tension and no stress,
In holidays, we do a lot of rest.

In holidays we go to many places,
Where we meet people of different races.

Really, holidays are very important for us,
As they free us from all sort of fuss.

Poetry

Poetry is an art through which we can describe everything,
And being an artist, it gives us wings.

It makes our mind very creative,
And also makes us intelligent and motivated.

It makes us happy and makes us proud,
So it makes us different from the common crowd.

It embellishes our inner beauty,
And protects us from being gloomy.

It presents us in a unique way in the world,
As it enables us to fly in the sky of success like a bird.

It can make us Shakespeare or Ruskin bond,
And can mould our life as we want.

I hope I will continue this spirit,
It will make me a good person, this is what I predict.

Painting

Painting is my love and not only an art,
This is the only way to express our love on the chart.

Painting does not have any limitation,
As it depends on our imagination.

Painting can help us to express our feelings,
Because for an artist a single dot also has a meaning.

We can paint everything that we want,
Like a tiger or my beautiful aunt.

Painting makes our mind stress free,
As it fills out heart with natural glee.

Painting can give us everything,
Like to reach our goals, it gives us wings.

Superpower Mind

Our mind is a superpower,
Which can help us to reach the success tower.

It makes us happy; it makes us sad,
It makes us feel good, it makes us feel bad.

It can make us corrupt or kind,
We can achieve everything, if we positively use our mind.

It never rest before completing its work,
And teaches us the lesson to never give up.

It can make us Newton and Einstein,
To reach that height we have to explore our mind.

Mind has also two sides,
One is wrong and one is right.

So choose always the right side,
As it can make our way bright.

I want

I want a dog for my fun,
I will play with it, when my work will be done.

Now I want a Labrador Retriever,
Because it has not much fur.

I and my brother will take it for a walk,
So, we will have a long morning and evening talk.

I promise, I will take care of it.
Though, I know it will trouble me a little bit.

I will give it everything like a cheesy bun,
Enjoying that food, we will have a lot of fun.

Dogs are with us till the end,
Because they are man's best friends.

I want (Part 2)

I want a room of my own,
In which I can sit all alone.

I want to have many ice creams,
But I know this will just remain my dream.

I want to be a Superman,
So that I can take the shape of anything like a coffee can.

I want to fly high in the sky,
But I can't, as I'm afraid of height, and
I will cry.

I want to be like a tiger,
Too much stronger and too much wiser.

I know it is difficult to fulfil these dreams,
But I can, if I will make it enjoyable as an ice cream.

www.ingramcontent.com/pod-product-compliance
Lightning Source LLC
LaVergne TN
LVHW050548160826
845677LV00011B/2226

* 9 7 8 9 3 9 0 4 4 6 7 2 8 *